Contents

Introduction 3

The Creation Plan of God 11

God Oriented Life 17

The Prophet Muhammad 23

The Sacred Texts 31

The Five Pillars of Islam 37

The Spirituality in Islam 51

WHAT IS ISLAM

Maulana Wahiduddin Khan

D1301470

Introduction

Everything in the universe—the sun, the moon, the stars— have all completely subjugated themselves to God's will; they cannot make the slightest deviation from the path He has ordained for them. Similarly, all other elements in nature function in obedience to the laws of nature laid down for them by the Creator. The entire universe has surrendered to God, the Lord of the Universe.

But there is a difference between the status of man and that of the physical world. The physical world has been given no option but to submit to God, whereas man has been given free will, so that he may opt for either good or bad ways. To this end he has been given a thinking faculty, and a conscience with which to make moral judgements for himself. He has the ability to accept and reject in order to follow certain principles in life. He is not bound by fixed laws like all other created beings. He has been given freedom of thought, option and action.

It is through this liberty of choice that man is being tested. But after being given a thinking faculty, a conscience and an ability to judge between good and bad ways, he was not just left to his own resources. God did not just leave man in a world where there was no way to find the truth. Divine provision for him went much further than that. To see how God gave His guidelines to mankind, we have to go right back to the beginning of creation. He took Adam, the first man—whom He had made not just an ordinary mortal but also a prophet—and taught him everything that He wanted from man, so that human beings would not be left without proper direction or guidance. From time to time thereafter, He sent large numbers of prophets to the world—the

◀ The Quba Mosque, Madinah.

last of these being the Prophet Muhammad—so that human beings, who tended to stray, could be recalled to the path of virtue.

Belief in God

Suppose we placed a pebble on a potter's wheel, and then spun the wheel around very fast. The pebble would, of course, fly off, even although a potter's wheel can hardly reach a speed of 25 miles an hour. Now, just think for a moment that the earth we live on is also revolving but at a much faster rate than the potter's wheel. Yet we do not fly off. The earth spins continuously on its axis at a speed of 1000 miles an hour—much faster than the average passenger plane—yet we move around on its surface, and live our daily lives without any fear of being thrown off like the pebble from the potter's wheel. What a miracle this is. The explanation scientists give us is that the earth pulls us with great force from underneath, while the pressure of the atmosphere from above pushes us firmly to the ground. A force attracting us from below, and a five-hundred mile thick blanket of air enveloping us from above are miracles enough in themselves, and to say that they explain our not flying off into space is to lend even greater credence to the miraculous nature of our entire world.

"Islam" is an Arabic word which means "submission, surrender and obedience to God."

Everything in this world, is, in fact, a miracle. Just think what happens when we put tiny seeds into the ground. The soil in which they are planted is uniform in constitution, but they bring forth a vast array of plants radishes, carrots, turnips, guavas, mangoes, mustard plants- everything indeed from the humblest blade of grass to the mightiest oak. Each plant has its own distinct appearance, taste and fragrance, and, according to its species, gives certain benefits to mankind.

On all sides of us, a whole world of miraculous diversity and proportions stretches out before our eyes. Moreover, at every instant, a great variety of life forms are continually coming into existence, quite unaided by man. Yet if all of the human beings in this world were to come together, they would not be able to create even one tiny grain of sand. This all amounts to a miracle of such amazing proportions, that words fail us when we have to describe it. When we try to do so, we only degrade it, for we are unable to do justice to it with mere human words. All we can do is look on in wonder, and ask ourselves: "Besides God, who could have made manifest such a miracle?"

Miracles All Around Us

Everything in this world is made up of atoms. In its final analysis, every object is a collection of these tiny particles. Yet by some strange miracle, when these atoms come together in certain proportions, they form the dazzling globe of the sun, and when the same atoms accumulate elsewhere in different proportions they flow in cascades: in yet other places, they take the form of subtle breezes or are fashioned into fertile soil. All these things may be made up of the same atoms, but the nature and properties of each separate object are widely different.

On all sides of us, a whole world of miraculous diversity and proportions stretches out before our eyes. Yet if all of the human beings in this world were to come together, they would not be able to create even one tiny grain of sand.

This miraculous world provides man with endless resources which he puts to good use whenever he learns how to tap them. Massive supplies of whatever he needs in life are constantly being accumulated, and man himself has to do very little in order to avail of them. Take, for instance, the food that he eats. He has but to stretch out his hand for the huge quantities of valuable nourishment which, as part of the order of the cosmos, has been made available to him. Once he has it in his possession, all he has to move are his hands and his jaws so that the food should reach his stomach. Then without any further effort on his part, the food is absorbed by the body and is turned into flesh, blood,

bones, nails, hair and other parts of the human body. Where food keeps the human body going, petroleum, another great earthly phenomenon, keeps his activities going. All man has to do is to extract it from the ground, refine it, put it into his machines and, astonishingly, this liquid fuel keeps the entire mechanism of his civilization running smoothly. Countless resources of this type have been created in this world, and there is enough of everything to meet man's needs. Man's part in bringing these things into being, or in changing them into some useful form, is a relatively small one. Therefore, with the minimum of effort, he has his clothes, houses, furniture, machines, vehicles and all the other components and accessories of his civilization. Are such occurrences not sufficient to prove that there is indeed a Maker and a Master of this world?

The earth rotates unceasingly in two ways—on its own axis and in orbit around the sun. But it does not create any noise in the process. A tree goes to work in the way of a great factory, but it does not emit any smoke. Daily, innumerable creatures are dying in the sea, but they do not pollute the water. The universe has been running in accordance with the divine order for billions of years, without ever having to reorganize itself, for everything about the way it is organized is so perfect. There are countless stars and planets moving around in space: they keep to the same speed, never lagging behind, and never exceeding their set pace. All these are miracles of the highest order. They are far more wonderful than anything that man can create, and they happen every instant in this world of ours. What further proof do we need that the power of a Great God lies behind this world?

The Signs of God

When we look at the different life forms, we witness an astonishing spectacle. Certain material objects come together in one body, and there comes into being a creature like a fish swimming through water, or a bird soaring in the skies. Of the great variety of creatures which abound on the earth, the one of greatest interest to us is Man. In ways that are a mystery to us, he is moulded into a well-proportioned form. The bones within him take on the meaningful shape of the skeleton, which is covered with flesh and sealed in by a layer of skin, out of which sprout hair and nails. With blood coursing through channels within this frame, all of this adds up to a human being who walks about, holds things in his hands, who hears, smells, tastes, who has a mind which remembers things, accumulates information, analyses it and then expresses it in speech and in writing.

The formation of such an amazing being from inert matter is more than a miracle. The particles of which a man is composed are the same as that of earth and stone. But have we ever heard a piece of earth talking, or seen a piece of stone walking around? The word miraculous is barely adequate to describe the capabilities of man. But what else is there to this walking, talking, thinking, feeling man which distinguishes him from earth and stone? This factor life- is still a mystery to us: there must indeed be a superior Being who has imbued inert matter with this quality, thus accomplishing a unique feat of creation.

Man has only to think of the nature of his own being to understand the nature of God. The self, the ego in man, has an individuality of its own, which is quite distinct from that of others of his kind living here on this earth. The ego in man is absolutely sure of its own existence. It is the part of man which thinks, feels, forms opinions, has intentions and puts them into practice. It also decides for itself which course of action to take.

> One who has found God has found everything. After the discovery of God, no further discovery remains to be made. God, for him, becomes a treasure which he cherishes, and it is to Him then that he has recourse for all his worldly and eternal needs.

Every human being is thus a separate personality with a will and power of his own. Since our experience of such a being is an every day matter, what is astonishing about the existence of God, who also is a being wielding personal power, although on a scale far greater than ourselves? Believing in God is a very similar mental process to believing in one's own self. That is why the Quran says that man himself is ample evidence for himself, however much he may excuse himself (75: 14-15).

People demand some miraculous proof before they will believe in the truth of God and His message. But what further proof do they require when they have the miracle of the whole of the universe which has been functioning perfectly for millions of years on the vastest of scales? If the doubter is not prepared to accept such a great miracle, then how is he going to shed his doubts when he sees lesser miracles? In truth, man has been provided with everything he needs to enable him to believe in God, and then to place himself at His service. If, in spite of this, he does not believe in God, and fails to acknowledge God's power and perfection, then it is he himself and not anyone else who is to blame.

Finally, the Discovery of God

One who has found God has found everything. After the discovery of God, no further discovery remains to be made. Thus, when a man has discovered God, his entire attention is focussed upon Him. God, for him, becomes a treasure which he cherishes, and it is to Him then that he has recourse for all his worldly and eternal needs.

God's world is a collection of atoms. In its elemental form, it all consists of one and the same type of inert matter; but God has moulded this matter into countless diverse forms: light, heat, greenery, flowing water. He has also invested lifeless matter with the properties of colour, taste and smell; and everywhere, He has set things in motion, having carefully controlled this motion by gravity. Discovering the God who has made such a world is much more than just acquiring a dry creed; it means filling one's heart and soul with the radiant glow of divine light and opening one's mind to incredible beauty and delicacy.

When we eat delicious fruits, this gives us a great sense of enjoyment. When we hear beautiful music we are quite entranced by it. When a handsome child is born to a couple, their joy knows no bounds. Then what of our experience of God, who is the source of all beauty, joy and virtue? On discovering Him, can one remain unmoved? This is something which is hardly imaginable, for such a sublime experience—like coming close to a source of dazzling radiance—must surely leave its mark on one.

Having endowed things with their unique qualities, God Himself must have qualities that His discoverers may savour. To discover Him, therefore, is to experience Him like a fragrance in the nostrils, a taste which excites the palate, a texture which is a joy to caress, a melody which touches the heart. To come close to Him is to live in an everlasting garden of brilliant colours and delicate fragrances. It is to hear such music that one might wish its enchantment to last forever.

The Creator of all light, God Himself is the most resplendent of all beings. He is the light of the Heavens and of the earth, shedding His radiance on the personalities of all who discover Him. His is the greatest treasure house of all true wisdom. He is the greatest repository of all true strength. His discoverers are so fortified by His strength and so enlightened by His wisdom that no flood or hurricane can carry them away. They cannot, once having known Him, do other than evolve into superior human beings.

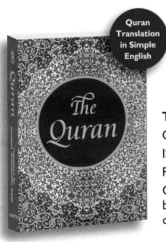

Wisdom and Insights in a Handy Quran

The Quran

Gift Edition (Size : 8 cm x 11 cm)

ISBN: 978-81-7898-735-4

Pages: 675

Copies of the Quran and other publications can be ordered online at www.goodwordbooks.com or call: +9111-24356666, 41827083

The Creation Plan of God

A western philosopher has written that it appears that man is a strange creature in this vast universe. It seems that neither man is made for this world, nor this world is made for man. Man and the Universe both seem to be a mismatch for each other.

Man is born with unlimited potentials. But in this present world, he finds only a very limited use of his potentials. Man, according to his nature desires to have an eternal life but very soon death arrives without his permission and finishes him off on a unilateral basis. Man carries unlimited desires within him, but these desires of his are never fulfilled.

World of dream is cherished by every man but these dreams are never realized. In this matter, there is no difference between the poor or rich, the big or the small. In the words of the philosopher mentioned above it seems that man has come to a world which was not made for him.

Why is man and the present world, are not in accord with each other? To find the answer of this question, we have to know the Creation Plan of God. This question arose due to unawareness of the creation plan only by knowing the creation plan of God we can arrive at a convincing answer.

The reality is that God—the Creator of man, has created man according to His plan. To become acquainted with this plan is necessary for a man to have a thorough understanding of himself—just as the workings of a machine can only be understood when we study the drawings of the engineer who made it. Without the knowledge of engineer's plan, nothing else can clarify the significance of that machine. Same is the case with man. The creator of the man has created him under a special plan. The plan is that man has to spend a trial period in this present unidealistic world, and after this, according to his deeds, he earns his right to inhabit the ideal world, another name of which is "Paradise".

◄ The Alhambra Palace courtyard in Granada, Spain.

The present world is a trial world. Here, any man and woman, to prove their worthiness for an entry into paradise, has two great parts: to acknowledge the truth and a disciplined life. Any man or woman who qualify themselves fully in this test, shall find a place in the ideal world of paradise. And those who fail in this test shall spent their lives in eternal deprivation.

Are We Completely Free?

Man finds himself completely free in this present world, but this freedom is not as his right instead it is a test paper for every one. What Man has to do is that without any pressure applied to him he acknowledges the truth. Without any compulsion he surrenders before the truth. He restricts his freedom by his own choice. To surrender oneself before the truth is without doubt the greatest sacrifice for any man. To acknowledge the truth is, apparently, to make oneself smaller as compared to others but this is the thing which shall gives man the highest position. It will guarantee his entrance into paradise.

In this connection, the second important thing is a disciplined life. Generally, man's character is moulded by his emotions—anger, revenge, jealousy, hatred, rivalry etc. These are negative perceptions which shape up the personality of a man. But a man should opt for a life of principle. He should not build his character under the influence of external incentives, rather his character should be based on principles. He, of his own will power must shape up his personality in the lights of sublime principles. This is the thing which is known as heavenly character.

Man has been created under the plan of creation. Man is the most noble creature of this entire universe. The existence of man is such a unique existence that no other example can be found in this vast universe. Man is rightly called as the most superior of the created beings. That is, the best and most meaningful being among all the created things.

The Hereafter

Those huge masses of ice, which we know as icebergs, found floating in the seas of the North and South poles, number amongst the most deceptive and, therefore, the most dangerous phenomena to be found in nature. Their deceptiveness lies in the fact that no matter how huge, or wonderful in configuration, what we see of them amounts to only one tenth of their enormous bulk. What lies below the surface of the ocean spreading far and beyond the visible perimeter, poses tremendous hazards to the unwary. In some ways, our lives are like those floating mountains of ice. The part we spend in this world—about a hundred years, or less— is like the part of the iceberg which is visible above the surface. We can see it, touch it, feel it. We can take its measure and deal with it effectively. But the part which comes after death is like the submerged part—vast, unfathomable and fraught with peril. It is something which defies the imagination, but which we must nevertheless try to comprehend, for that is the part of human life which God has decreed should be eternal and, as such, ineluctable.

We are all familiar with the facts of our origin and the course which life takes from the womb until death. But at the end of our lifespan, whether it terminates in youth or in old age, our familiarity with the nature of things comes to an end. It has been surmised that death means total and final annihilation. But this is not so. Death is simply a means of consigning us to a new womb, to the womb of the universe itself. From that point, we are ushered into another world: the Hereafter. While the present, physical world as we know it has a finite time-frame, the Hereafter stretches away from us into infinity. We fondly imagine that there is some parallel between the pleasures and pains of this world and those of the next, but, in truth, nothing that we can experience in this world will ever match the extremes of agony and bliss of the life after death. Those who merit punishment in the Hereafter will be condemned to suffer the most horrific pain for all time to come. But those who merit God's blessings in the Hereafter shall know the most wonderful joy and contentment.

> Man has been created under the plan of creation. Man is the most noble creature of this entire universe. The existence of man is such a unique existence that no other example can be found in this vast universe.

It is because life in this world is intended to be a

testing-ground that the world of the Hereafter remains beyond our reach. But all around us, we have innumerable signs which can help us, by analogy, to understand and appreciate the nature of the world to come. Imagine a room which ostensibly consists of four walls, furniture, a few material objects and some human occupants. To all outward appearances, that is what the room adds up to. But the moment we switch on the TV set, we are introduced to a hitherto unsuspected world of colour, movement, and highly vocal human activity. This world, with its scenery and very alive human beings, had existed all along. It had only needed the flip of a switch to make us aware of it. Similarly, our terrestrial existence is made up of a world within a world. The world we know is concrete, visible, audible, tangible. The 'other' world, the world within it, or rather, beyond it, is not, however, one which can be apprehended through any of the normal human senses; no switch can be turned on to make us understand what it is really like. Only death can do this for us. And, when we reopen our eyes after death, we find that what had formerly been impalpable, and quite beyond human comprehension, is now a stark, overwhelming reality. It is then that we grasp what had hitherto existed, but had remained invisible.

What is Success?

Once we have become clear in our minds that the afterlife truly exists, we realize that the sole aim of our earthly existence should be to strive for success in the life to come, for, unlike the present ephemeral world, the Hereafter is eternal and real. What we understand by suffering and solace in this world cannot be compared with the suffering and solace of the Hereafter.

Many individuals lead immoral, even criminal existences because they feel that we are free to do as we please in this world. Freedom we do have, but it exists only so that God may distinguish between the good and the evil, and determine who deserves a place of honour and dignity in the Hereafter and who should be condemned to eternal disgrace. While there is nothing to prevent the good and the evil from living cheek by jowl in this world, they will be separated in the Hereafter like the wheat from the chaff, and will be judged in strict accordance with their record in this life. Some will be condemned to an eternal Hell of pain and distress, while others will be blessed with eternal bliss and pleasure. Each will ineluctably get his deserts.

Two men once brought a case before the Prophet for judgement. One had misappropriated the other's land, but because of certain legal quirks, it was difficult to pass a verdict against him. After due consideration, the Prophet warned him: "If the court gives a verdict in your favour, think of it as being fire and brimstone which you have been awarded." The piece of land might, in terms of this world, have been a prized possession, but in the perspective of the Hereafter it would assume the terrible properties of fire and brimstone.

What we understand by suffering and solace in this world cannot be compared with the suffering and solace of the Hereafter.

These two sides of human deeds have been beautifully described through allegories and symbols in the *hadith* of the *mi'raj* (The Prophet's Journey to the Heavens). When the Prophet reached *Sidrah al-Muntaha* (the lote tree at the end of the Seventh Heaven), he saw four rivers: two flowing inward and two flowing outward. It was explained to him by the angel Gabriel that the two inward-flowing were rivers of Paradise, and the outward-flowing were the Nile and the Euphrates.

By analogy, the present world and the Hereafter are two sides of the same event. The worldy side is trivial and temporary, while the Hereafter side is substantive and permanent. It is to the latter side that we must face up after death. Here one has complete freedom to live out one's worldly texistence as one wills; in the life-to-come, one will have no choice about the future course of one's life. One will either be raised to eternal glory, or cast down into the pit of everlasting Hell.

God Oriented Life

The Earth is the sun's satellite. It constantly orbits around the sun. It takes one year to complete such a rotation. This movement of the earth around the sun is essential for the healthy functioning of life on earth. If the earth did not revolve around the sun, its existence would have no meaning, and life would come to an end.

This is a practical example of how we should lead our lives in this world. This example is indeed a physical demonstration that shows how man must revolve around God, just as the earth revolves around the sun. It means that all of man's activities should be based on God.

The earth rotates as compelled to by the laws of nature. But man, of his own free will, should surrender to God. He should build a life, which is based on the concept of God. This consciousness is the real ascension of man. In this consciousness lies the secret of all success. A God-oriented life begins with the discovery of God. When individuals, whether men or women, discover God, it means that they have found the truth. And this truth pervades their whole being. This feeling of having discovered the truth becomes such a thrilling experience that it fills them with everlasting conviction. This everlasting conviction removes all frustrations from their lives. Therefore, losses are no longer such, for, in spite of them, they never lose the feeling that their greatest asset, i.e. God, is still with them.

Man experiences this realization by pondering upon God's creations. The present universe is an expression of God's attributes. It is a complete introduction to God. God is visible in His creations, just as clearly as a human being sees his own reflection in the mirror.

The vastness of space tells man that God, its Creator, is boundless.

◀ The Dome of the Rock, Jerusalem.

The observation of the sun and the stars shows us that God is all light. The heights of the mountains show us the greatness of God. The waves of the sea and the flow of the river tell us that God is a storehouse of boundless blessings. We see God's bounty in the greenery of the trees. Man's existence becomes a proof of God's existence. In the waft of air he experiences a Divine touch. In the chirping of the birds, he hears God's songs.

For man, a God-oriented life starts by his remembering God. He begins to feel the presence of God. Everything serves to remind him of God. God's remembrance is never absent from his heart and mind. His mornings and evenings are spent as if he is living in God's neighbourhood. Just as rain replenishes the crops, so does he remain ever immersed in the remembrance of God.

The Source of Spiritual Development

God is a spiritual focus for man. One whose heart is attached to God undergoes spiritual experiences at every moment. Belief in God becomes a source of spiritual development for him. Filled with the love of God, he does not need anything further. God becomes a vast ocean for him to continue to swim in without ever experiencing any limit. In the form of spiritual awakening, he receives such great wealth that he does not feel any need for anything else.

For one who discovers God, the entire universe becomes an open book of God for him. Every leaf of a tree becomes a page of the divine book.

When he sees the sun, he feels as if God is lighting His heavenly torch so that he may read His book clearly. The Universe becomes, as it were, a supernal university and he its student.

Finding God is to find his centre of Love. Man by birth is a seeker of a Supreme Being who is far above him, who is free from all limitations and who may form the centre of his feelings, in short, a Being after finding whom a grown man becomes as satisfied as a child after being held in the arms of his mother. This discovery of God saves one from regarding something other than God as God and mistakenly and unrealistically thinking it to be the answer to the urge inherent in his nature. The discovery of God is to fulfill his or her real urge to find God. And the failure to discover God means failing to find that which is man's greatest need.

One who fails to find God is compelled by his natural urge to give the place of God to something other than God. This place is sometimes accorded to a certain human being, sometimes to a certain animal, sometimes to a phenomenon of nature, sometimes to a certain material power, sometimes to a certain supposed concept and sometimes just to the self.

Even if one fails to discover God, or he becomes a denier of God, it is not in his or her power to stifle the urge in his nature to find God. That is why those men and women who have not found God inevitably come to hold something other than God as God. And this supposed God is always some creature or the other of God. By nature, it is possible for man not to accept the real God as God, but it is not possible for anyone to save himself or herself from granting the status of divinity to something other than God. Making God one's object of worship raises man's position. On the contrary, regarding something other than God as God amounts to descending from the level of humanity. Submission to God is the only way of life for both man and the universe.

The present universe is an expression of God's attributes. It is a complete introduction to God. God is visible in His creations, just as clearly as a human being sees his own reflection in the mirror.

God's Prophets

The Islamic concept of prophethood is different from that of other religions. Some religions would have it that even God Himself becomes incarnate in human shape, and that his prophets are in some way superhuman or other-worldly. But a prophet in the Islamic sense is no different from any other human being. His uniqueness lies simply in his being the chosen messenger of God.

God's prophets were born into this world just like any other

human beings. They led their lives just as others did, thus demonstrating to their people how God's servants should, in practice, conduct themselves on earth, and showing them clearly what path they must tread in order to avert God's displeasure and make themselves worthy of His blessings.

Man has been placed on this earth by God in order that his obedience to his Creator may be put to the test. For this purpose he has been given complete freedom to tread the paths of both good and evil. He has a choice. But to follow the path desired for him by God, man is in need of guiding principles. The true source of guidance, according to Islam, is to be found in prophethood. Throughout human history, God in His infinite mercy selected certain individuals to communicate His message to mankind, so that all human beings might be given an opportunity to follow the right path. These chosen people were called prophets, or messengers.

God's prophets were born into this world just like any other human beings. They led their lives just as others did, thus demonstrating to their people how God's servants should, in practice, conduct themselves on earth, and showing them clearly what path they must tread in order to avert God's displeasure.

A prophet is a person chosen by God as His representative. When God appoints someone as His Prophet, He sends His angel to him to inform him of his new status. In that way, the individual can have no doubts about his appointment as God's Prophet. Later, God reveals His message to him through His angels, so that he may communicate the divine teachings to all his fellow men.

God has given man a mind so that he may be endowed with understanding. But this mind can only grasp things that are apparent. It cannot go below the surface, and there are many things to be apprehended, for which a superficial knowledge is insufficient. The deeper realities of this world are beyond the scope of the human mind, and so far as God and the next world are concerned, they must remain forever invisible—beyond the reach of human perception.

What the Prophet does is to enlighten people so that they may overcome this human inadequacy. He tells of the reality of things here and now, and also gives tidings of the next world. He thereby enables the individual to formulate a plan for his entire existence in the full light of knowledge and awareness so that he may carve out a successful life for himself.

Have you considered the water that you drink? Is it you who cause it to descend from the clouds, or do We? If We so pleased, We certainly could make it salty. Why, then, are you not grateful?
The Quran
56: 68-70

O God, only You can change our hearts. We beseech You to do so, so that we may submit to you.
The Prophet Muhammad

Among the best of you are they who have the best character
The Prophet Muhammad

We shall show them Our signs in the universe and within themselves, until it becomes clear to them that this is the Truth. Is it not enough that your Lord is the witness of all things?
The Quran
41: 53

Be humble and do not harm or consider yourself superior to others.
The Prophet Muhammad

The Prophet Muhammad

Poised between Africa, Asia and Europe, the Arabian peninsula lay at the very heart of the ancient world. Yet no ambitious conqueror had invaded the territory; no ruler had sought to bring it under his domain. All military campaigns had been limited to the area bordering Arabia, Iraq, Syria, Palestine and Lebanon. As for the Arabian peninsula, no one had considered it worth fighting for. True, its shores were lapped by three seas, but its interior offered little beyond inhospitable desert and barren mountains.

The Early Years

Makkah was the central township of this land, it was in this "uncultivable valley" in which it lay that the Prophet Muhammad, on whom be peace, was born on 22 April A.D. 570. His father, 'Abdullah ibn 'Abdul Muttalib, died a few months before the birth of the Prophet. He was only six years of age when his mother, Aminah, also passed away. For two years he was cared for by his grandfather, 'Abdul Muttalib, and, when he too died, the Prophet's uncle, Abu Talib, became his guardian. Abu Talib's demise occurred three years before the emigration of the Prophet to Madinah. The Prophet then, at the most difficult stage of his life, was left without a protector. But nature had endowed the Prophet with a remarkable personality. Those who saw him in his youth used to remark: "This boy has a great future."

As he grew up, the nobility of his personality used to have an effect on anyone beholding him, but he was so soft-spoken and

of such genial disposition that anyone coming into close contact with him would learn to love him. A perfectly balanced personality—tolerant, truthful, perspicacious and magnanimous—he presented the highest example of human nobility. He became known as he grew older as the most chivalrous among his people, tolerant and forebearing, truthful and trustworthy, always the good neighbour. He would stay aloof from all quarrels and quibbles and never indulged in foul utterances, abuse or invective. People even left their valuables in his custody, for they knew that he would never betray them. His unimpeachable trustworthiness won for him the title of *"al-Amin,"* a faithful custodian, an unfailing trustee.

Search for the Truth

His inborn high qualities had impressed the richest woman in Makkah, Khadijah, a forty-year-old widow belonging to a family of merchants. When the Prophet was twenty-five, she offered herself to him in marriage. Not only did marriage with Khadijah provide the Prophet with wealth and property; it also threw open to him a vast field of business in Arabia and beyond. The Prophet had every opportunity, then, of leading a successful and comfortable life. But he forsook all these things and chose something quite different for himself. Quite intentionally, he took a road that could lead only to worldly ruin. Before his marriage, the Prophet had earned his living in different ways. Now he relinquished all such activity, and dedicated himself to his lifelong vocation—the pursuit of truth. He used to sit for hours and ponder over the mysteries of creation. Instead of socializing and trying to gain a position for himself among the nobles of Makkah, he would wander in the hills and dales of the desert. Often he used to retire to the loneliness of a cave in Mount Hira'—three miles from Makkah—and stay there until his meagre supply of food and water was exhausted. He would return home to replenish his supplies, and then go back to the solitude of nature for prayer and contemplation. He would beseech the Maker of the heavens and the earth for answers to the questions surging in his mind. What is our true role in life? What does the Lord require of us, as His servants? Whence do we come and whither will we go after death? Unable to find answers to these questions in the centres of human activity, he betook himself to the stillness of the desert; perhaps, there, the answer would be forthcoming.

This reality is discovered not merely on an intellectual level. When it takes root, it transforms one completely, and raises one's level of existence. The Prophet Muhammad provides us with a superlative example of this way of life.

God, indeed, relieved him of his burden. He turned His mercy to His Prophet, illuminating his path and guiding him on his journey. On February 12, A.D. 610, the Prophet was sitting alone in his cave. The angel of the Lord appeared before him in human form and taught him the words which appear at the beginning of the ninety sixth chapter of the Quran. The Prophet's quest had finally been rewarded. His restless soul had joined in communion with the Lord. Not only did God grant him guidance; He also chose Muhammad as His Prophet and special envoy to the world. The mission of the Prophet extended over the next twenty-three years. During this period the entire content of the Quran—the final divine scripture—was revealed to him.

The Prophet Muhammad discovered Truth in the fortieth of his arduous life. It was an attainment that was not to usher in ease and comfort, for this Truth was that he stood face to face with an Almighty God. It was discovery of his own helplessness before the might of God, of his own nothingness before the supernatural magnitude of the Almighty. With this discovery it became clear that God's faithful servant had nothing but responsibilities in this world; he had no rights.

The meaning that life took on for the Prophet after the Truth came to him can be ascertained from these words:

Nine things the Lord has commanded me.
> Fear of God in private and in public;
> Justness, whether in anger or in calmness;
> Moderation in both poverty and affluence;
> That I should join hands with those who breakaway from me;
> and give to those who deprive me;
> and forgive those who wrong me;
> and that my silence should be meditation; and my word remembrance of God;
> and my vision keen observation.

These were no just glib words; they were a reflection of the Prophet's very life. Poignant and wondrously effective words of this nature could not emanate from an empty soul; they themselves indicate the status of the speaker; they are an outpouring of his inner being, an unquenchable spirit revealed in verbal form.

In other words, this is how God's faithful servant passes the day. Sometimes the yearning of his soul brings him so close to God that he finds something in communion with the Lord. Sometimes fear of the day when he will be brought before the Lord for reckoning makes him reckon with himself. Sometimes he is so overawed by the marvels of God's creation that he starts seeing the splendours of the Creator reflected therein. Thus he spends his time encountering the Lord, his own self, and the world around him, while also finding time to cater for his physical needs.

These words are not a description of some remote being; they are a reflection of the Prophet's own personality, a flash from the light of faith that illuminated his own heart. These "moments" were an integral part of the Prophet's life. One who has not experienced these states can never describe them in such a lofty manner. The soul from which these words emanated was itself in the state that they describe; through words that state of spiritual perfection was communicated to others.

Before he received the word of God, this world—with all its

shortcomings and limitations—appeared meaningless to the Prophet. But now that God had revealed to him that besides this world there was another perfect and eternal world, which was the real abode of man, life and the universe took on new meaning. He now found a level on which his soul could subsist, a life in which he could involve himself, heart and soul. The Prophet now found a real world into which he could put his heart and soul, a target for all his hopes and aspirations, a goal for all his life's endeavours.

This reality is discovered not merely on an intellectual level. When it takes root, it transforms one completely, and raises one's level of existence. The Prophet Muhammad provides us with a superlative example of this way of life.

The greatest lesson imparted by his life is that, unless one changes one's plane of existence, one cannot change one's plane of actions.

When the Prophet Muhammad discovered the reality of the world hereafter, it came to dominate his whole life. He himself became most desirous of the heaven of which he gave tidings to others, and he himself was most fearful of the hell of which he warned others. Deep concern for the life to come was always welling up inside him. Sometimes it would surge to his lips in the form of supplication, and sometimes in the form of heartfelt contrition. He lived on a completely different plane from that of ordinary human beings. This is illustrated by many incidents a few of which are mentioned here.

The Prophet Muhammad discovered Truth in the fortieth of his arduous life. It was discovery of his own helplessness before the might of God, of his own nothingness before the supernatural magnitude of the Almighty. With this discovery it became clear that God's faithful servant had nothing but responsibilities in this world; he had no rights.

This is what is meant by the world being a planting ground for the hereafter. One who realizes this fact lives a life oriented towards the hereafter—a life in which all efforts are aimed at achieving success in the next, eternal world; a life in which real

value is attached—not to this ephemeral world—but to the life beyond death.

But the Prophet's whole life was moulded by thoughts of the hereafter. He loved his children, but not in any worldly way. 'Ali ibn Abi Talib, Fatimah's husband, once told a story about the Prophet's most beloved daughter. "Fatimah's hands," he said, "were blistered from constant grinding; her neck had become sore from carrying water; her clothes would become dirty from sweeping the floor." When the Prophet had received an influx of servants from some place, 'Ali suggested to his wife that she approach her father and ask for a servant. She went, but could not speak to the Prophet because of the crowd. Next day, the Prophet came to their house, and asked Fatimah what she had wanted to see him about. 'Ali told the Prophet the whole story, and said that he had sent her. "Fear God, Fatimah," the Prophet said, "Fulfill your obligations to the Lord, and continue with your housework. And when you go to bed at night, praise God thirty-three times, and glorify Him the same number of times; exalt His name thirty-four times, and that will make a full hundred. This would be much better than having a servant." "If that is the will of God and His Prophet," Fatimah replied, "then so be it." This was the Prophet's only reply. He did not give her a servant.

The truth revealed to the Prophet was that this world did not spring up by itself, but was created by one God, who continues to watch over it. All men are His servants, and responsible to Him for their actions. Death is not the end of man's life; rather it is the beginning of another, permanent world, where the good will enjoy the bliss of paradise and the wicked will be cast into a raging hell. With the revelation of this truth also came the commandment to propagate it far and near. Accordingly, ascending the height of the rock of Safa, the Prophet called the people together. First he made mention of the greatness of God. Then he went on to say:

By God, as you sleep so will you die, and as you awaken so will you be raised after death: you will be taken to account for your deeds. The good will be rewarded with good and the evil with evil. And, for all eternity, the good will remain in heaven and the evil will remain in hell.

The basic principle of the Prophet's teaching mission was that emphasis should be laid entirely on matters pertaining to eternity. Under no circumstances was his teaching to dwell on worldly issues. The true issue confronting man is that of his eternal fate. All other issues are transitory and superfluous. Worldly success and failure have no meaning, for they are bound to end. It is on the next world, where success and failure will be abiding, that man should focus his attention.

Furthermore, it was the Prophet's aim to build a society of upright individuals, and such a society can only be formed if each separate individual behave with moral rectitude. True and consistent morality can come only from a profound belief in the hereafter. Belief in the hereafter means that we are not free to act as we please but that we will expect to be taken to task for our actions by God. It rids one of wayward attitudes and makes one into a disciplined and responsible human being. If one reads the Quran and Sayings of the Prophet with an open mind, one will find that it is the life after death which receives most attention. Other matters are mentioned, but only incidentally. The fundamental purpose of the Prophet's mission was to concentrate people's attention on the hereafter.

> The basic principle of the Prophet's teaching mission was that emphasis should be laid entirely on matters pertaining to eternity. Under no circumstances was his teaching to dwell on worldly issues. The true issue confronting man is that of his eternal fate.

The Sacred Texts

The Quran

The Quran is a book of revelations from God. Today it exists in the form of a book consisting of 114 chapters. They were sent down by the angel Gabriel or Jibril, bit by bit according to the demand of circumstances. The Quran is a revealed book: it is not authored by a human being. It is the actual word of God in human language. The Quran began to be revealed to the Prophet Muhammad through the angel Gabriel, in A.D. 610, while the Prophet was sitting in seclusion in the cave of Hira at the top of the Mountain of Light, two miles from Makkah. Thus the scriptures were not revealed in book-form at one point of time. Their various parts were revealed as the occasion demanded. It was later compiled in Madinah during the last days of the Prophet. The entire revelation was completed over a period of 23 years. The last passage was revealed to the Prophet while he was addressing a gathering at Mount Arafat after performing his last Hajj in A.D. 622.

Themes of the Quran

The main theme of the Quran is to make people aware of the Creation Plan of God. According to this divine plan, man was created as an eternal being. The Creator divided man's life into two parts, pre-death and post-death. The pre-death period is that in which man is

◀ A young boy reads from the Quran at a mosque in Jeddah.

put to the test. The post-death period is that in which he will be rewarded or punished. The former is temporary, while the latter will last for all eternity.

The Quran aims at bringing about an intellectual revolution in every human being. All its teachings are therefore spiritual in nature. All its verses address the human mind, their main thrust being to promote contemplation on nature, for which the Quranic words are *tafakkur, tadabbur* and *tawassum*. The Quran, in effect, strives to promote spiritual behaviour and peaceful conduct in national as well as international life.

According to Quranic teachings, violence has no place in human life. Although Islam gives freedom to all, this comes with the proviso that this freedom should be exercised without resorting to violence. If an individual is peaceful in intent and conduct, he is allowed to exercise his freedom as he wills.

All the basic tenets of spirituality, ethics, and peaceful behaviour are laid down in the Quran in very clear terms. But the Quran is not a book of law; it is a book of reflection. Moreover, the Quran presents as a model of Quranic conduct the Prophet Muhammad. The Prophet, who lived a full life, followed Quranic teachings in all aspects of his practical behaviour. If one wants, therefore, to have an understanding of the tenets of the Quran, he may refer to the Quran and one who wants to become acquainted with the model of this Quranic conduct may study the life of the Prophet Muhammad, which is known as *sirah*.

Regarding the multi-religious society, the Quran is very practical. It gives the following formula: For you your religion, for me mine. In other words: Follow one and respect all. This formula is based on the well-known principle of peaceful coexistence indeed, the only way of existence in this world.

Regarding social life, the essence of Islamic teaching is that God has granted freedom to everyone. This freedom in itself demands that people should lead their lives with restraint. Because, if freedom is exercised without restraint, it will inevitably result in clash and breakdown, destroying social life in their wake.

The most repeated invocation in the Quran is "In the name of God, the most Beneficent, the most Merciful." The occurrence of this invocation 114 times in the Quran is in itself an indication of how important it is. Every piece of work must have a beginning. It is the Quran's desire that when one initiates any undertaking one should begin by uttering the name of God. One is thus always reminded of God's attributes of benevolence and compassion.

The teaching of the Quran can be summed up under two basic headings: (1) Oneness of God: believing in One God and worshipping Him alone; (2) Brotherhood of Mankind: regarding all human beings as equal and according equal rights to all. These two kinds of precepts can be expressed as monotheism and justice.

Compassion for Humanity

The aim of the Quran—with its 6000-plus verses spread over 114 chapters—is to develop a man who would possess the two sublime qualities of being a worshipper of God and a well-wisher of mankind. According to Quranic philosophy, human life is intertwined with God and mankind. On the one hand is God, his Creator, and on the other are human beings among whom he has to lead his life from the moment of his birth until his death. The Quran encourages man to have sublime feelings for God and to reflect these sentiments in the way he worships Him. At the same time, it is made clear to him that in his heart he must also have feelings of benevolence and compassion for humanity at large. To be a true Muslim requires a combination of these two virtues.

The Quran emphasizes the formation of one's character through introspection and moulding oneself to the will of God. Nowhere does it enjoin the believer to engage in violence, leading to the destruction of fellow human beings.

The Quran tells us that God has given innumerable blessings to humanity. Man, as he benefits from this divine bounty, is duty-bound to offer thanks to his Benefactor. He is bidden to love and fear God more than anyone or anything else, and ought to consider himself accountable.

The Quran emphasizes the formation of one's character through introspection and moulding oneself to the will of God. Nowhere does it enjoin the believer to engage in violence, leading to the destruction of fellow human beings.

The Quran tells us, moreover, that the present world is intended to be a testing ground, specially designed for the trial of mankind, for God wants to see whether people are capable of leading their lives in accordance with His will. It is their conduct on earth that will determine whether or not they are deserving of Paradise in the next, eternal stage of life after death.

According to the Quran, Paradise is another name for God's neighbourhood, and in this neighbourhood only those who are sincere in their belief in God and have compassion and love for God's servants will find acceptance.

God has the same compassionate relationship with every man as a father has with all his children. Therefore, it is alien to the divine scheme of creation that this earthly plane should be marred *by* hatred, killing and violence. It is God's most cherished desire that love should be returned for hatred, and violence should be met with peace.

The Hadith and Sunnah

Hadith, meaning a "statement" or "report", is used as an Islamic term for the records kept of the sayings and doings of the Prophet Muhammad. *Sunnah* means the actions the Prophet himself performed, or actions he asked his followers to perform. The Hadith is a record of the *Sunnah*.

Hadith provides the second fundamental source of Islam, giving us a full account of the life of the Prophet, and serving as a commentary on the Quran.

The Quran principally deals with basics. It is the Hadith which gives the details and necessary explanations of Quranic injunctions. For instance, the Quran says: "Establish the service of worship." But it does not specify how the worship has to be performed. Not even the timings and units of prayers (*rak'ahs*) are clearly mentioned. We need the traditions set forth in the Hadith to have full information on this.

Even after knowing the details, it might still not have been possible to follow the divine injunctions contained in the Quran. For not everything can be properly understood by words alone. Therefore, the Prophet demonstrated to the faithful how prayer was to be performed. He said to the believers: "Look at me, see how I worship, and follow me."

The Quran repeatedly reminds us of the importance of Hadith, enjoining us to strictly follow the Prophet:

"...Obey God and obey the messenger..." (*Al-Nisa*, 4:59).

It is as if the Quran is the text and the Hadith the commentary, the Quran being the theory and the Hadith the practice. The Quran and Hadith are complementary to one another and are thus inseparable. Both are equally essential for the establishment of religion.

The contemporaries of the Prophet are known as the Companions, or *sahabah*. Because the Companions believed in the message of the Prophet, all his actions served as a precedent for them and every word falling from his lips became a commandment to them; and they were anxious to follow each one as faithfully as they could. During the lifetime of the Prophet Muhammad, many of his Companions learnt by heart whatever he said, and keenly observed whatever he did, all of which they shared with each other. They naturally thirsted after the knowledge of what he said or did, so that many, like Abu Hurayrah, Anas ibn Malik and Abdullah ibn Mas'ud, kept constant company with him in order to observe and hear his every word and deed. Aishah, the Prophet's wife, was the first among women to tell of the Prophet's sayings and doings. She reported more than two thousand *hadith*, while Abu Hurayrah related more than five thousand *hadith*.

Hadith, meaning a "statement" or "report", is used as an Islamic term for the records kept of the sayings and doings of the Prophet Muhammad. *Sunnah* means the actions the Prophet himself performed, or actions he asked his followers to perform. The Hadith is a record of the *Sunnah*.

Later, the sayings were compiled by various collectors of *hadith*. In this regard, Bukhari and Muslim are the first to have applied the most rigorous measures to ascertain the reliability of each *hadith*. An unbroken chain of narrators was traced for each *hadith* and each transmitter's life was analysed from all angles to validate his trustworthiness.

The Five Pillars of Islam

The Prophet Muhammad has said, "Islam has been built on five pillars: testifying that there is no god but God, and that Muhammad is the Messenger of God; saying prayers; paying the prescribed charity (*zakat*); making the pilgrimage to the House of God in Makkah and fasting in the month of Ramadan."

Although a building is composed of many parts, what really holds up the entire structure is its pillars. If they are strong, the whole structure will be sound. But should they be weak, the entire edifice will crumble. Those which support the edifice of Islam are of immense strength, but they must first of all be raised up by its adherents if they are to support its structure.

Man's life is like a piece of land on which he must build a house to God's liking. His first step must be to set up these five sturdy pillars, without which Islam cannot raise itself up either at the individual or at the community level. These five pillars— faith, prayers, fasting, charity and pilgrimage—are meant to engender in man a lifelong piety and devotion to God.

Faith *(iman)* means belief in divine truths. Prayer, in essence, means bowing before the glories of God, so that any sense of superiority a man may have will be dispelled. Fasting *(sawm)*, with its emphasis on abstinence, builds up patience and fortitude. Charity *(zakat)* entails the recognition of other's needs, so that what has been given to mankind by God may be equitably shared. Pilgrimage *(hajj)* is a great rallying of God's servants around Him. These are not mere empty rituals, but the exercise of positive virtues, the quintessence, in fact, of those

◀ The Kabah in the Sacred Mosque, Makkah.

qualities which our Lord wishes to be inculcated in us. If we can cultivate them, we shall be deemed to possess the divine characteristics so cherished by Islam. Thus it is true to say that faith, humility, fortitude, recognition of the rights of others and unity are the pillars on which rests the entire edifice of Islam.

Faith (Iman)

Acceptance of God as one's Lord is like making a covenant to place Him at the central point in one's life, so that He may become the pivot of one's thoughts and emotions. It means entrusting oneself to Him entirely, and focussing upon Him all one's hopes and aspirations, fears and entreaties. Then, instead of living for worldly things, one will live for one's Sustainer. He will thus become all in all in one's life.

Man all too often live for worldly things which come to dominate his thoughts and emotions. Some live for their household and family; some for business and the money it brings; some for political activity and party leadership, and some for honour and authority. Every man, big or small, lives for something or the other which is material in this everyday world of ours. But this is to live in ignorance—trying to build one's nest on branches that do not exist. A truly worthy life is that which is lived for one's Lord, with no support other than Him. Man should live in remembrance of God. His name should be on his lips as he wakens and as he sleeps. As he halts or proceeds on his way, he should live in trust of God, and when he speaks or remains silent, it should be for the pleasure of his Lord.

The Essence of Faith

Faith in God is like the electric current which illuminates the whole environment and sets all machines in motion.

When a man finds the link of faith to connect him to God, experiences just such an illumination from within sudden and all-embracing. His latent spirit is then awakened and his heart is warmed by his new-found faith. A new kind of fire is kindled within him. Man, born of the womb of his mother, has his second birth from the womb of faith. He now experiences what is meant by union with God. A lover, emotionally, is one with his beloved, even when he is physically separated from the object of his love. In this state, he sees in everything the image of the loved one. One who is inspired by his faith in God is just like this earthly lover. He sees the glories of God in heaven's blue vaults, and His might and grandeur in the fury of tempests. The birds, with their twittering, seem to warble hymns to God. The rising sun is the radiant hand of God extending towards him. Every leaf of every plant and tree is a verdant page on which he reads the story of divine creation. Zephyrs fanning his cheeks are harbingers of his unity with God. A true believer in God is like a diver in the divine ocean. Every plunge that he makes serves to unite him in his experience more and more inextricably with his Maker, so that he belongs to God as God belongs to him.

The Prophet Muhammad has said, "Islam has been built on five pillars: testifying that there is no god but God, and that Muhammad is the Messenger of God; saying prayers; paying the prescribed charity (zakat); making the pilgrimage to the House of God in Makkah and fasting in the month of Ramadan."

Faith in God means faith in a Being who is at once Creator, Master and Sustainer of all creation. Everything has been made by Him and Him alone, and receives eternal sustenance from Him. There is nothing which can exist without Him. Consciousness of this and faith in God go hand in hand. As a consequence, a man of faith begins to look upon himself as a servant of God. In each and every thing he witnesses the glory of God, and every blessing he receives strikes him as a gift from God; hymns to the deity and remembrance of God spring from his heart like fountains. He lives,

not—in forgetfulness, but in a state of acute awareness, all events being reminders to him of God. When he awakens from a deep and refreshing sleep, he begins involuntarily to thank his Lord for having blessed man with sleep, without which he would be in such a perpetual state of exhaustion that life, brief as it is, would become hellish for him and drive him to madness. When the sun rises high in the sky and sends its light to the world, dispelling the darkness of the night, his heart cries out in ecstasy, 'Glory be to God who created light. Had there been no light, the whole world would be a fearful ocean of darkness.' When, driven by hunger and thirst, he eats and drinks, his entire being is filled with heartfelt gratitude and, bewildered and amazed, he asks himself: 'What would become of men if there were no God to send us food and drink?' When in need, or if he is hurt, he looks towards God, calling upon Him for succour. When he encounters adversity, he accepts it as part of God's design, and if he is fortunate enough to earn profits or, in some other way, finds himself at an advantage, he is reminded of God's blessings and his heart is filled with gratitude. His achievements do not, however, fill him with conceit, nor do his failures crush him or even make him impatient. In all such matters, whether of loss or gain, his adoration of God is never impaired, nor does anyone or anything other than God ever become its object. No expediency ever makes him forget his Lord.

The discovery of the power of gravity on earth and on other bodies, or of radiation in the universe with the help of sophisticated instruments, is an achievement of an academic nature with no overtones of religious compulsion. But the discovery of God is an entirely different phenomenon. It is the direct apprehension of a Being who is all-seeing and all-hearing, and who is the repository of all wisdom and might. Discovering God means, moreover, acceptance of the fact that God has not created man, or the universe at large in vain. That a magnificent universe should stand mute, without its true significance ever being understood and appreciated, is inconceivable when its Creator and Sustainer is an all-knowing God.

Man's discovery of faith instills in him the conviction that a day must come when the unseen God—the great orchestrator of all events in the Universe—will make Himself manifest, so that man will see and believe tomorrow what he fails to see and, therefore, questions, today. His belief tells him that the manifestation of the Creator and Master will be like the brightness of the sun after the darkness of the night—the manifestation, indeed, of an omniscient Judge and Arbiter.

Prayer (Salat)

Prayer, the second pillar of Islam, entails the worship of God five times a day in the prescribed manner. This mode of worship, laid down for mankind by God through His Prophet, is so all-embracing that one cannot imagine any superior way of worshipping the Almighty.

Acceptance of God as one's Lord is like making a covenant to place Him at the central point in one's life, so that He may become the pivot of one's thoughts and emotions. It means entrusting oneself to Him entirely, and focussing upon Him all one's hopes and aspirations, fears and entreaties.

When the time for prayer comes, the greatness of God is proclaimed in the call to prayer, and the faithful are instructed to assemble for prayer as a matter of their own spiritual uplift. They then perform their ablutions—in so doing reviving their sense of cleanliness—and, fixing their minds on God, they make their way to the mosque, where they all offer prayers together. The prayers are led by an Imam, under whose guidance Muslims are shown how they should lead their lives. In the same way as the congregation make the Imam their leader in prayers, so should all Muslims unite around the Prophet, making him the focal point of their social existence.

The prayer has various stages: bowing low, prostrating oneself, and standing and kneeling before God. In assuming these various postures, the congregation demonstrate their submission to the Lord. When they stand, hands joined in prayer, when they bow low, when they sit reverently before the Lord, when they touch the ground with their foreheads, with each posture they adopt, they renew their covenant of submission to God.

During the prayers, an excerpt from the Quran is read out. One amazing attribute of the Quran is that, no matter which part is chosen and how much of it is recited, its message is clearly conveyed. This

is because each page of the Quran is like a summary of the whole. In this way, any short excerpt from the Quran recited in prayer suffices to show what pleases and what displeases the Almighty.

Besides this, the prayers include praise and remembrance of God, supplications to Him and the expression of goodwill towards the Prophet and all believers. The prayers then end with a message of peace to all mankind. Thus constituted, they are both an act of worship and a reminder of God's commandments. They give solace to believers, while creating social consciousness and unity in their ranks. Prayer is not only a symbol of the Islamic life, but also inculcates self-discipline among Muslims. Although the most important aspect of prayer is its being the main point of spiritual contact with God, it also has valuable lessons for us on how to conduct ourselves in our daily lives.

Prayer, as well as being a ritual mode of worship, is an expression of the inner realities' of humility before, and devotion to God. The ultimate acknowledgement of another's greatness being the repetition of the words, "He is the Greatest," the words, *Allahu Akbar,* are uttered time and time again in prayer. Verbal acknowledgement is thus made of the absolute quality of God's greatness in comparison to that of ordinary mortals.

Physically, the ultimate recognition of another's greatness is the act of self-prostration; no physical act is more obviously a testament to the greatness of another than this. Performed repeatedly during prayers, it is a practical reminder and a clear demonstration of one's belief in the incomparable grandeur of God. The giving of one's entire attention to God is underlined by turning one's gaze towards the House of God. The direction in which one must face in order to pray is, therefore, of great religious significance, for it not only focuses one's attention on the deity, but also demonstrates that one's very life is turned towards God. Every aspect of one's life, from inner thoughts to outer needs, then becomes truly God-oriented.

The Spirit of Humility

When a servant of God bows before his Lord, and does so, not just as a matter of form, but in the spirit of true humility, the effect of his action does not remain confined to the domain, but extends to his everyday existence, pervading it completely. His thinking and actions bear the permanent stamp of his devotions, for it is impossible for

Prayer, as well as being a ritual mode of worship, is an expression of the inner realities' of humility before, and devotion to God. The ultimate acknowledgement of another's greatness being the repetition of the words, "He is the Greatest," the words, Allahu Akbar, are uttered time and time again in prayer. entreaties.

a man to fear God and to bow before Him without being influenced thereby in his dealings with others. A true worshipper cannot be humble and meek before God and yet be arrogant and supercilious to his fellow men. He will not, of course, prostrate himself before them, nor will he address the words "You are great" to another person, as he would to God. But he will certainly avoid asserting his own superiority, and instead will adopt a humble demeanour on a parallel with his self-prostration before his Maker. The submission which he expresses in prayer to God becomes a reality in terms of his observance of others' rights. The very act of facing in the correct direction influences him to take a principled stand in his everyday dealings. At prayer in the mosque, he is the epitome of servitude to God: outside the mosque, he is the perfect character—humble in demeanour, morally upright, and kind considerate and forgiving in all his transactions.

The important thing about prayer is that it induces the correct attitude in the devotee, as though the spirit of his prayers were keeping a watchful eye on everything he says and does. When going about his worldly affairs, it is as if the whole world were a mosque; his actions, therefore, at all times and in all places cannot be other than in consonance with what his worship requires of him.

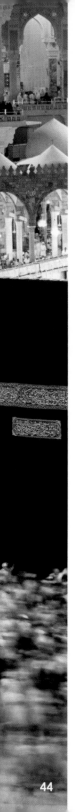

Fasting (Sawm)

Fasting (sawm) is the third pillar of Islam. Right from dawn till dusk, a man who is strictly on a fast will neither eat so much as one morsel of food nor drink so much as one drop of water. By submitting to this discipline, that is, by depriving himself of the prime necessities of life, he learns the valuable lesson of fortitude. With no food and drink, he naturally feels hungry and thirsty, and his strength begins to ebb. The entire routine of his life is severely disturbed and his whole system is upset. But, out of a high sense of discipline, he braves all these difficulties and discomforts, and, remaining alert and never losing heart, he steadfastly discharges his duties. Food and drink may be temptingly placed before him, but, despite an overwhelming urge to have both, he will not even touch them. In this way, he prepares himself for a well-regulated and responsible life, doing only what is his duty and refraining from pernicious acts and habits. He is thus strengthened to continue with his mission in life, no matter how he may be beset by adversity.

God has endowed man with innumerable gifts, but, all too often, he takes them for granted without any feelings of gratitude. Countless benefits like the air, the sun, the water, have been showered upon man, the absence of anyone of which would cast his delicately balanced system into a living hell. But because he has received these things without any effort on his part, he sets no great value upon them, and hardly ever stops to ponder upon how they came to be his.

It is only when fasting temporarily curbs the satisfying of his desires that his consciousness of the value of these divine gifts is awakened. When, at sunset, after a whole day's hunger, thirst and the accompanying discomfort and fatigue, a man begins to eat and drink, he becomes fully aware of his utter dependence on God's bounty. He is then filled with gratitude towards God and the realization comes to him that, even were he to lay down his life for this

Bountiful Creator, the price he should have to pay would not be too high.

The life of a believer in this world is one of fortitude and forbearance, limited as it is to the enjoyment of whatever is allowed by God and avoidance of whatever is forbidden by Him. It will naturally be beset by all the difficulties encountered in the path of righteousness and truth, and the believer must staunchly face up to them. Much of his time must be given to such activity, and no precious moment can be wasted in stooping to revenge himself upon adversaries who have made him the object of their spite and malice. On the contrary, the slights and injuries of this world should leave him undaunted; he should be able simply to take such untoward incidents in his stride so that he may continue unflinchingly to discharge his duties. Whenever his pride has been hurt, or whenever some unpleasantness has left him in a state of agitation, he must guard against adopting a negative attitude—for this is sheer weakness!—and must continue to devote his energies in a positive manner to worthy objectives. Nothing, in fact, should stop him, or even slow him down in his progress towards the Hereafter.

The annual month-long period of fasting builds up the strength of character which is essential, if devout believer are to tread the path of righteousness for the rest of the year, avoiding impatience, cruelty and all such evil acts, and making no attempt to meddle with divine commandments.

All of this demands enormous fortitude, and, without it, no one can travel along the path of Islam. The annual month-long period of fasting builds up the strength of character which is essential, if devout believer are to tread the path of righteousness for the rest of the year, avoiding impatience, cruelty and all such evil acts, and making no attempt to meddle with divine commandments. While in its outward form, fasting means abstinence from food and drink for a given period, in essence, it is training for a whole life of self-denial, inculcating patience, fortitude and forbearance.

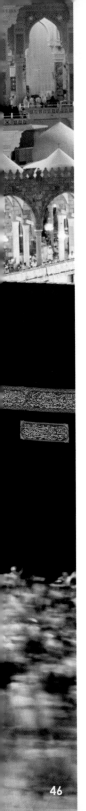

The Prescribed Charity (Zakat)

Zakat is the fourth 'pillar' of Islam. *Zakat* means setting apart for God every year a certain portion of one's saving and wealth (generally 2.5 percent) and spending it upon religious duties and on poor and the needy. The fulfilment of this duty is, in fact, a kind of reminder that all one has is in trust for God. Man should, therefore, hold nothing back from God. To whatever one may amass in one's lifetime, one's own personal contribution is insignificant. If the Supreme Being, who is at work in the heavens and on the earth, refused to co-operate with man, there would be nothing that the latter could accomplish single-handed. He would not be able to plant so much as a single seed to make things grow. Nor could he set up any industries, or carry out any other such enterprise. If God were to withdraw anyone of His material blessings, all our plans would go awry, and all our efforts would be brought to naught.

Zakat is the practical recognition of this fact through the expenditure of money. Islam requires man to consider his personal wealth as belonging to God and, therefore, to set apart a portion for Him. No maximum limit has been prescribed, but a minimum limit has definitely been fixed. According to statutory *zakat,* each individual must abide by this and spend a fixed minimum percentage of his wealth every year in the way prescribed by God. In so spending his wealth, he is permitted neither to belittle the recipient nor to make him feel obliged or grateful to himself. His wealth must be given to the needy in the spirit of its being a trust from God which he is making over to the genuine titleholders. He should feed others so that he himself is fed in the Hereafter, and he should give to others so that he himself is not denied succour by God in the next world.

Zakat is a symbol of one's obligation to recognize the rights of others and to be in sympathy with them in pain or in sorrow. These sentiments should become so deep-rooted that one begins to regard one's own wealth as belonging, in part, to others. Moreover, one should render service to others without expecting either recognition or recompense. Each individual should protect the honour of others without hope of any gain in return. He should be the well-wisher of not just friends and relations, but of all members of society. *Zakat,* first and foremost, makes it plain to people that their entire 'possessions' are gifts of God, and, secondly, dissuades the servants of God from living in society as unfeeling and selfish creatures. Indeed, throughout their entire lives, they must set aside some portion for others.

Zakat is a symbol of one's obligation to recognize the rights of others and to be in sympathy with them in pain or in sorrow. These sentiments should become so deep-rooted that one begins to regard one's own wealth as belonging, in part, to others.

One very wrong way of conducting oneself in any social set-up is to live in expectation of worldly gain from the services rendered to others. An example of such behaviour is to lend money in the hopes of getting it back with interest. Where this is a common practice, exploitation becomes rampant, with everyone trying to subjugate and plunder others. As a consequence, the whole of society is plagued with disorder.

No one, be he rich or poor, can be happy in such a set-up. If a man is correctly motivated, he will be of service to his fellow-human beings only in the hope of receiving a reward from God: he will give to others with the divine assurance that he will be repaid in full in the next world. In a society where there is no exploitation, feelings of mutual hatred and unconcern cannot flourish. A climate of mutual distrust and disorder is simply not allowed to come into being; each lives in peace with the other, and society becomes, a model of harmony and prosperity.'

On the legalistic plane, *zakat* is an annual tax, or duty, in essence and spirit: it is recognition on the part of man of the share which God, and other men, have in his wealth.

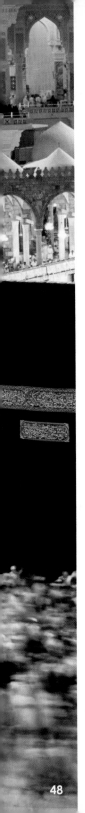

The Pilgrimage (Hajj)

The fifth pillar of Islam is pilgrimage or Hajj. On this occasion, believers from all corners of the earth gather together at Makkah, and perform the various prescribed rituals in worship of God. These are symbolic representation of those qualities which according to Islam, it is imperative that we personally cultivate. They are a concretization in different visually appreciable forms of the dictates of Islam—a physical affirmation to God that man will organize the moral structure of his life on the same pattern. Although these particular elements are inherent in other modes of Islamic worship, in Hajj, they are more pronounced, more comprehensive and altogether on a grander scale.

One very important obligation during Hajj is the wearing of unstitched clothing *(ihram),* for it is inconsistent with Islam that the material distinctions of clothing should set up artificial barriers between the servants of God. Dressed in this way, all men of all countries look alike in identical, simple garments, and no pilgrim may then feel tempted to take pride of place over another.

In Islam, man's life must rotate around God. Circling the holy Kabah is but a symbolic representation of this. Similarly, running between Safa and Marwa, two hillocks of the region, gives physical expression to the Islamic precept that the true servant of God should come running at his bidding, that he should have an overwhelming feeling of urgency about carrying out God's commandments. The vocal affirmation of man's desire to bow to God's will is the repetition of the words, *'Labbaik allahumma labbaik'* (Here I am, O Lord, Here I am.) The assembling of the pilgrims on the vast plains of Arafat is an impressive visual reminder of the day when according to Islam, all men will be assembled before God. On the score of wanting man to be intolerant of the devil, Islam is quite positive, and the casting of stones at the symbolic figures of 'Satan' gives physical expression to this striving to ward off evil. Perhaps the greatest Islamic imperative is that man should be steadfast in his covenant with God, even at the cost of life and property. The material expression of his adherence to this covenant is the symbolic sacrifice of animals in Mina.

Islam has always set a great value upon social harmony. In order, therefore, that all discord should be eliminated, much emphasis is placed upon the individual's ability to ignore the malevolence of others. The Hajj period, with its assembly at one place of a heterogeneous crowd running into millions, provides a special occasion for the exercise of such self-discipline. It has been ordained then for the duration of the Hajj period, when there are bound to be occasions for grievances, that anger, foul talk, fighting, injury to living things, obscenity or dishonesty will not be indulged in by anyone. God's servants must treat each other with respect and decency if they expect to have God's blessings.

Hajj is a complete lesson in leading a God-oriented life. In that it reminds one of the awesome day of Resurrection—a day that could be painful for many—it is a prelude to the attainment of God, exhorting us to strive with all our might to tread the path of righteousness. It warns man that! Satan is his arch-enemy and that he should never allow him to draw near. It conveys the message that if we are anxious to receive the bounties of God, we should be ready to sacrifice our lives and property for His sake. A grand demonstration of the equality of man, it provides a situation in which being able to bear the disagreeable behaviour of others, and living together in an atmosphere of amity and goodwill, are of paramount importance.

> Hajj is a complete lesson in leading a God-oriented life. In that it reminds one of the awesome day of Resurrection—a day that could be painful for many—it is a prelude to the attainment of God, exhorting us to strive with all our might to tread the path of righteousness.

Hajj, in a nutshell, is a complete mode of worship which, if performed in the correct manner, will have a transfiguring effect upon the moral aspects of the affairs of man, be they worldly or religious in nature.

The Spirituality in Islam

According to the Quran spirituality resides in the mind, and is achieved at a purely intellectual level. The Quran uses several terms to express it: *tawassum, tadabbur* and *tafakkur* meaning drawing lessons through reflection, thinking and contemplation.

All things around us, from a tiny blade of grass to the vast Milky Way, and from the trees, plants and mountains to the sun, the moon and the sky—all are silent reminders of the greatness of the Creator. Everything that exists on this planet or in the universe is an amazing artistic marvel extolling the magnificence and magnanimity of the great Creator.

Spirituality is the elevation of the human condition to a plane on which the mind is focused on the higher, non-material realities of a godly existence. Spirituality in Islam is an intellectual activity. Its quest is two-fold; *one* is to give serious thought to questions pertaining to their purpose of life such as, "Who am I?" What is this world around me? What is the creation plan of God for man as well as for the rest of the world? And *two* is to solve the riddle of why all men and women undergo negative experiences in this world and to offer positive solutions.

The inner transformation of mind and soul translates into outer spirituality blessed with peace and blissfulness. The spirituality of one who is spiritual on the inside will also reflect on the outside. Peace inside will radiate peace outside. Such a person will become more content, tolerant and respectful towards others. Anger, jealousy and negativity will be converted into a positive attitude which radiates forgiveness and compassion and, instead of thrusting his viewpoint on others, he will be more considerate and understanding. He will talk less and listen more. Instead of pointing out the faults in others, he will spend his time in introspection. His focus will be on his duties rather than

◀ The Sehzade Mosque, Istanbul, Turkey.

on his rights. He will live as a harmless individual, contributing to society in positive and meaningful ways.

It is, therefore, the responsibility of every individual to uplift himself spiritually and realise the Creator. And then lead his life in accordance with God's creation plan. The main reasons for them not doing so are their forgetfulness of the Hereafter, and their obsession with worldly pursuits.

Then man lives his life in the remembrance of God. He begins to feel the presence of God. Everything serves to remind him of God. God's remembrance is never absent from his heart and mind. His mornings and evenings are spent as if he is living in God's neighbourhood. Just as rain replenishes the crops, so does he remain ever immersed in the remembrance of God.

The concept of God in Islam provides man with an ideology in which loss is turned to gain and in which adversity brings with it good tidings. And it is in submission to God and living a God-oriented life that man finds complete fulfillment and purpose of life. When he discovers God and worships Him, when he remembers Him, when his mind is turned towards Him with full concentration, when he makes a request or a plea, he establishes a contact with his Creator. In the words of the Hadith, at that particular moment he comes to whisper with his Lord. He has the tangible feeling that he is pouring his heart out to God and that God in turn is answering his call.

This is the beginning of living a God-Oriented Life and the development of a positive personality. It is, therefore, in submission to God that man and the rest of the universe find its purpose. While the rest of the world submits to God compulsively, without having a choice; God desires that man should submit to Him of his own free will, without being compelled to do so. This is the test of man. When man submits to God and starts living a God-oriented life based on the principles of life laid down by his Creator, he starts developing his personality on positive lines and becomes a purified soul. It is souls such as these, who, in the life Hereafter, will inhabit paradise. Our most compassionate Lord will say:

"O soul at peace, return to your Lord,
well-pleased, well pleasing.
Join My servants;
Enter My Paradise."

Maulana Wahiduddin Khan is an Islamic spiritual scholar who has adopted peace as the mission of his life. Known for his Gandhian views, he considers non-violence as the only method to achieve success. Keeping this ideal consistently before him, he has written over 200 books on Islam and a commentary on the Quran. His most recent publication is *The Prophet of Peace: The Teachings of the Prophet Muhammad* (Penguin Books). Internationally recognized for his contributions to world peace, he has received, among others, the Demiurgus Peace International Award, the Padma Bhushan, and the Rajiv Gandhi National Sadbhavna Award.

Watch
Maulana Wahiduddin Khan
on ETV Urdu
Monday to Thursady
at 5:00 a.m.

CPS International, the Centre for Peace and Spirituality is an organization, which aims to promote and reinforce the culture of peace through mind-based spirituality. Non-profit-making and non-political in nature, it is engaged in promoting peace and spirituality through inter-faith efforts. Drawing inspiration from the Quran, the preserved word of God, and the Sunnah, the sayings and actions of the Prophet Muhammad, the Centre seeks to share the spiritual principles of Islam with the world and to reveal its true face, based as it is on peace, tolerance and co-existence.

The sphere of action of CPS is global and every peaceful method is being used to address the modern, scientific thought of young people and inquisitive minds of all ages.

For more details, you can access the following websites, get involved with our mission and spread the message of peace and mutual understanding:

www.cpsglobal.org   **www.alquranmission.org**
www.alrisala.org   **www.goodwordbooks.com**

CPS International
1, Nizamuddin West Market, New Delhi - 110013
Mobile: +91-9810558483, Fax: +91-11-45651771
email: info@cpsglobal.org www.cpsglobal.org

Center for Peace and Spirituality USA
2665 Byberry Road, Bensalem, PA 19020
Office: (215) 240-4298, Cell: (617) 960-7156

30 Isernia Ave., Staten Island, NY 10306
Office: (718) 477-6090, Cell: (718) 715-3600
email: cps@alrisala.org www.alrisala.org

Join hands with the CPS to make world peace a reality!

Books by Maulana Wahiduddin Khan

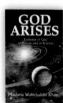
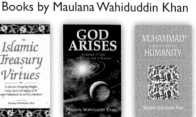

Made Simple Series

Madinah Arabic Reader

Professor Abdur Rahim's textbooks enable the student to acquire a knowledge of Arabic in the classical structural form.

General Islamic Subjects

Arabic Learning

Quran and Quranic Studies

Hadith and Sirah

Quran & Hadith Trivia

The daily calendar is loaded with a treasure-trove of useful information.

Moral Values for Children

Help your children imbibe Islamic moral values through simple text and vivid illustrations.

A Treasury of Stories from the Quran & Seerah

The answers to every child's longing to hear a good bedtime story.

- A simple text
- Fabulous colour illustrations

The book offers a special dimension to these wonderful goodnight stories.

Islamic Games & Gift Boxes

Ideal gifting options for children

Islamic School Books

This course teaches young students comprehensive Islamic education, comprising general Islamic knowledge based on the Quran and Hadith.

New Releases...

Bringing you a Splendid Range of Islamic Books and Children's Products

Goodword offers innovative products for children, including Quran stories, moral stories, craft and activity books, gift packs, Islamic games, Arabic and Islamic readers for home and school. In addition to this, Goodword also offers a variety of Islamic books for adults, including English translations of the Quran, the Hadith, the life of the Prophet Muhammad, and books on Arabic learning and Dawah.

A complete catalogue of Goodword publications can be downloaded from Goodword's website.

We welcome you to our bookstore, it is open all seven days from 10 am to 8 pm.

Goodword Books
1, Nizamuddin West Market
New Delhi - 110 013, India
Mob. +91-8588822672
Tel.: +9111-24356666, 41827083
email: info@goodwordbooks.com
www.goodwordbooks.com

First published 2013
The text of this book is copyright free.
Picture Credits:
Getty Images: cover, 2, 10, 22, 30, 36, 50
Abdul Wahid Pedersen: 16
Rest of the images under license from 123rf.com
Printed in India